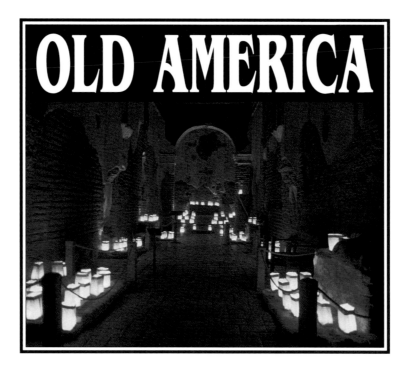

OLD AMERICA

Missions

Lynn Stone

Rourke Publications, Inc.
Vero Beach, FL 32964

Edited by Sandra A. Robinson

PHOTO CREDITS
© Steve Warble: cover, 4, 6, 9; © Frank Balthis: title page, 8, 10, 14, 15, 17, 19, 21, 23, 25, 27, 29; © James P. Rowan: 18; © Bancroft Museum: 12, 20.

Library of Congress Cataloging-in-Publication Data

Stone, Lynn M.
   Missions / by Lynn M. Stone.
   p. cm. — (Old America)
   Summary: Describes the missions built in America by the Spanish and examines their political, military, and religious significance.
   ISBN 0-86625-445-5
   1. Spanish mission buildings – United States – Juvenile literature. 2. Indians of North America – Missions – Juvenile literature. [1. Missions.] I. Title. II. Series: Stone, Lynn M. Old America.
E159.S795 1993
973.2—dc20   93-18638
                                                      CIP
                                                      AC

TABLE OF CONTENTS

I. Missions 4

II. Missions of the Southeast 12

III. Missions of the Southwest 15

IV. Missions of California 19

V. Life on the Mission 23

VI. The Spanish Padres 25

VII. Missions: A Tour 27

Glossary 30

Index 32

I   MISSIONS

The Spanish missions were islands of Spanish civilization in the wilderness of America.

Mainly because of a few adventurous and dedicated men, Spain left its cultural imprint on a large part of America. The men were Roman Catholic priests, mostly from the Order of Franciscan Monks. Their job was to establish missions, outposts of the Roman Catholic Church and Spanish civilization. There they could teach Native Americans about Christianity and Spanish customs. The missions were not always successful and many of the natives did not wish to convert to Christianity. Still, missions left a Spanish imprint on architecture, language, farming, food, place names and customs.

Spanish missions began to make their mark on American history more than 400 years ago. Back then, Spain was a powerful nation. She had a great navy and an even greater appetite — for wealth and land. Christopher Columbus was employed by Spain when he sailed to the New World in 1492. That voyage sparked a hunger in Spain and other European countries for the riches of the Americas.

After the voyage of Columbus and other explorations, Spain claimed huge chunks of North America. In those days, that's all it took to own a country or two — a voyage, a flag in the sand and a speech by the ship's captain. It was finders-keepers. The only people living in America then were the Native Americans. They had "discovered" America many years before Columbus. The white man did not recognize Native American

Spain sought to strengthen its land claims in America through missions such as San Xavier del Bac in Arizona.

claims to America — their interests and welfare didn't count for a whole lot.

Spain would never become rich from her land holdings in North America, but it wasn't for lack of trying. Spain clung stubbornly to parts of North America for 350 years. Until the early 1800s, Spain reigned over a large portion of southern North America, including much of what would become the United States.

Spain was not able to use and control all her land. She did not have a large population, so she could not send thousands of Spaniards to North America as **colonists**, or settlers. Yet she had to do something to keep the other European powers, especially England and France, from nibbling away at her possessions.

Spain's solution was a system of frontier missions. The center of a mission was a **quadrangle**, a four-sided arrangement of walls, walkways and other structures linked together. The walls were built basically to keep **hostile**, or unfriendly, natives out and to keep friendly natives in. Most of the missions were built of stone and **adobe** bricks. Within the quadrangle, which surrounded an open courtyard or plaza, were storerooms, shops, school rooms, living quarters, a church and other structures. Often, additional buildings stood outside the quadrangle. Missions also included lands around the quadrangle that were farmed by people from the mission center.

Spain thought her missions would make the New World natives loyal to Spain. By teaching the Spanish **culture** — including its language, customs, religion, and craftsmanship — Spain would make the New World a truly Spanish **colony**. Although far from Spain, the colony would have close ties to the homeland. The Spanish government thought that loyal natives would help Spain resist French and English attempts to overtake Spanish territory in North America. Curiously, the Spanish rarely allowed mission natives to carry weapons. As a result, they had no value as a fighting force.

Spain also wanted her missions to **convert**, or change, the religious beliefs of Native Americans to those of the Roman Catholic Church. Roman Catholicism was the national religion of Spain. In Spanish eyes, the natives

The distinct architecture of the Spanish missions was repeated in the walls and archways of other buildings throughout the Southwest and Southern California.

were uncivilized **heathens**, people who did not believe as they did in the God of the Bible. Spain believed that it was her moral obligation — the right thing to do — to make Christians of the natives in new Spanish lands. Making *Christian* natives, however, was less important to the Spanish government than making *Spanish* natives. "Spanish natives," loyal to Spain, would help Spain spread her influence in the New World.

The plan was that a mission would become self-supporting from its crops and the labor of the natives. In time, the mission would become a **pueblo**, or village. Then the missionary priests could move into new territory and build new missions. The missions, though, rarely followed the Spanish plan for them. Missions were destroyed by floods, fires, earthquakes,

Pecos National Historic Park in Pecos, New Mexico, preserves the ruins of this adobe mission church built in the 1700s.

The bright beauty and craftsmanship of mission churches,
such as this one at Mission San Miguel, California, appealed to
Native Americans.

native attacks and English settlers. As soon as a mission was abandoned, most of the Native Americans returned to their own tribal traditions and religions.

So for 250 years, beginning in the 1560s, Spain established missions in lands of the future United States. Priests and little bands of soldiers came northward from Spain's colonies in the Caribbean Sea and New Spain (Mexico). The missions sprouted first in Florida and Georgia. Later they were established, along with a handful of Spanish **presidios**, or forts, in the Southwest and California.

Native Americans in the missions sometimes participated in their own festivities after Catholic church services.

Spain established her first mission in America in 1565 at St. Augustine, Florida. She eventually planted another 40 missions in Florida and Georgia. Insects, hostile natives and the hot, humid climate made mission life difficult and dangerous.

Unpaid and often overworked, natives occasionally rebelled against their Spanish **overseers**. Diseases carried by the Spanish were dangerous to the native population. Hundreds of natives, on and off the missions, died from "white man's diseases" like measles, smallpox, cholera and tuberculosis. Yet many of the missions were fairly prosperous in the mid-1600s. Food production was high and the Spaniards claimed to have converted 30,000 Native Americans to Christianity. As Spain had feared, it was English settlers who would deliver a killing blow to the Spanish missions in the Southeast.

The English and Spanish had crossed swords in Europe. Now, in the 17th century, the old hatreds were carried by the two countries into the American Southeast. Like Spain, England claimed parts of the Southeast as hers. In order to weaken English claims, the Spanish were giving safe haven to runaway black slaves from English colonies. English traders and settlers, often with the help of Native American allies, attacked the Spanish missions and left them in ruin. Spain had neither the colonists nor the army to defend

Built of stone in the 1700s, Mission San Jose in San Antonio, Texas, was equipped with cannons to fight off raiding Comanches and Apaches.

her interests. By 1745, Spain held only a few Southeastern missions in northern Florida. In 1763, England took Florida from Spain. That ended Spain's frontier mission system in the Southeast.

III MISSIONS OF THE SOUTHWEST

An old stairwell at Mission Concepcion, part of St. Antonio Missions National Historic Park, Texas.

Spain first established missions in the American Southwest during the 1600s. She built missions in New Mexico, Arizona and Texas. As usual, Spain got little benefit from her investment in these missions. Nevertheless, they helped open the Southwest for settlement.

In 1680 the missions in New Mexico were under attack by the native population. A native leader named Popé organized a revolt of the Pueblo people. Natives killed more than 400 Spanish settlers and 21 priests, forcing the survivors into Texas.

Scattered missions survived in the Southwest until the late 1820s. By then, Spain's empire in the New World had fallen apart. For years the missions had faced a loss of government support and had suffered attacks by hostile natives. Mexico won her independence from Spain in 1821, and former Spanish territory in the Southwest and California became Mexico's. In 1833 Mexico began to take over ownership of the missions and their property in a process called **secularization**.

Shortly after the Mexican takeover, the Texas mission of San Antonio de Valero (better known as the Alamo) achieved lasting fame. At that time, it was no longer being used as a mission. On March 6, 1836, a large Mexican army under General Santa Anna attacked the Alamo and wiped out a 185-man force made up largely of Americans. The Americans had been working

According to legend, Rosa's Window at Mission San Jose was sculpted by a young Spaniard as a memorial to his girlfriend, who drowned at sea.

The rugged walls of the Alamo (Mission San Antonio de Valero) were defended by Americans and overrun by hundreds of Mexican soldiers on March 6, 1836.

for the independence of Texas. The courage of its defenders made the Alamo one of the most famous places in American history, and the battle one of its most famous events.

IV MISSIONS OF CALIFORNIA

Mission San Juan Capistrano is seen along its covered passageway, or arcade. Father Junipero Serra is known to have led Catholic services here 200 years ago.

The Mission of St. Gabriel in California, from a drawing by a 19th century artist.

Spanish missions came to California late in the life of Spain's empire. Spain claimed California in 1542, but she ignored this northern frontier until 1769, when Russia expressed an interest in it. Spain sent a few soldiers, settlers and padres, or priests, north into California from Mexico. With sword and cross, a network of missions and a few presidios established Spanish authority.

The leader of the missionary priests, Father Junipero Serra, was an exceptional man — able, selfless and courageous. Between 1769 and 1803, he and Father Fermin Lasuen founded 18 of California's 21 missions. The mission chain stretched about 700 miles, from San Diego north to San Francisco. When Mexico secularized California missions in 1834, there were more than

Native Americans in California often lived in their own homes on the mission site.

20,000 Christian natives in California. Mission properties were large, productive and generally peaceful. In part, it was the success of these missions that called the world's attention to California.

The end of the mission system in California was tragic for the natives. Perhaps they might have been better off without European culture in the first place, but the natives suffered greatly after the missions closed. Mexico divided some of the mission property among the natives. Not used to owning or managing land, many of them sold or gambled the land away.

California became United States property after the war with Mexico ended in 1848. The natives had begun to scatter after the missions were taken by Mexico.

Under the American flag, the situation became worse. Native rights and property were trampled upon by the wave of Americans who flocked to California during the gold rush of 1848-50. Natives died by the thousands — from bullets, alcoholism, disease and neglect. California's native population fell from 100,000 in 1848 to 30,000 in 1859.

V LIFE ON THE MISSION

Native Americans learned the Spanish way to spin and weave, as well as other Spanish crafts.

The Spaniards created a need in the native population for metalware, beads, fine clothing and blankets. By giving gifts to the curious natives, the padres earned their attention and sometimes their participation in mission life.

Natives who joined the mission agreed to take religious instruction, attend church services and learn Spanish customs. In return, the missions fed and clothed the natives and made sure they had shelter.

With good reason, the Spanish feared that natives who left the mission would return to their former ways. Therefore, the missions insisted that they remain on the mission unless they were granted permission to leave. The Spanish were teachers and disciplinarians. In their view, the natives were children.

VI THE SPANISH PADRES

*Mission San Juan Bautista was founded in 1797 by
Father Fermin Lasuen.*

Many Spanish padres were men devoted to teaching and helping Native Americans. They lived no better than the mission natives in their care. They risked danger in some of the most remote parts of America. Many of them died at their missions, far from home.

Many padres genuinely wanted to help the natives learn another way of life. Father Serra, for example, was excited by the idea of starting missions in the unknown wilderness of California. With a badly infected leg, he rode a mule 750 miles up the Baja California peninsula to begin his labor. At his mission headquarters he slept on a cot with one blanket. His room was furnished simply with a table, a chair, a storage chest, a candlestick and a **gourd.**

Some padres experienced the joy of bringing Christianity to the natives. Even so, they knew loneliness, disappointment and sadness. Native deaths were commonplace, and sometimes Christian natives left the mission and never returned.

A priest was a teacher, preacher and administrator. In addition to his normal duties, he often settled conflicts between natives and Spanish soldiers. The soldiers frequently abused the natives.

VII MISSIONS: A TOUR

Lamplight shows the path to Tumacacori Mission in southern Arizona.

Most of the surviving old missions have been **restored** — rebuilt and repaired to look as much like the originals as possible. Visitors find the grounds of old missions rich in history, as well as religious traditions.

Most missions have active churches and hold Catholic services. A few missions offer tours and schedule festivals on special days. At the Mission of San Juan Capistrano in California, the return of hundreds of cliff swallows is a highlight of each St. Joseph's Day, March 19.

Some of the missions stand today only as churches. Many of these are now crowded within cities. A few others still occupy open ground, just as all of them did long ago.

Here is a sampling of missions:

In New Mexico, San Esteban, one of the few churches to survive the Pueblo Revolt of 1680, stands high on a desert **mesa**. The ruins of the Mission of Nuestra Senora are in Pecos National Monument. Salinas Pueblo Missions National Monument protects four of America's six surviving 17th century mission churches. In Texas, San Antonio Missions National Historic Park holds four missions along the San Antonio River.

Tumacacori National Historic Park in southern Arizona is the site of a mission established in 1751. Beautiful San Xavier del Bac Mission is near Tucson.

Cattle hides dry at La Purisima Mission, a California state historical park where mission life is re-created by costumed interpreters.

California has 21 mission sites, each with its own fascinating story. One of the most impressive sites is in Carmel. La Purisima, carefully rebuilt, spreads across a valley. The only remaining church where it is known that Father Serra held services is at San Juan Capistrano.

GLOSSARY

adobe (uh DOE bee) - a bricklike material of straw and sun-baked earth

colonist (KAHL un ihst) - one who travels from one place to settle in another that is ruled by the person's native country, such as a colonist from Spain settling in the colony of New Spain

colony (KAHL uh nee) - a group of people who settle in a distant land but remain under the rule of their native country; the land settled by colonists

convert (kun VERT) - to change from one belief to another

culture (KUHL cher) - the beliefs, lifestyle and other characteristics of a society

gourd (GORD) - a squashlike vegetable that is sometimes dried and used as a container

heathen (HEE then) - to Christians, one who does not believe in the God of the Bible

hostile (HAHS til) - unfriendly

mesa (MAY suh) - an isolated hill with steep sides and a flat top

overseer (O ver see er) - one who is responsible for the smooth operation of a business; one who directs others and their activities

presidio (pri SID ee o) - Spanish army post

pueblo (PWEB lo) - a Native American village in the Southwest; a specific tribe of Southwestern Native Americans (Pueblo)

quadrangle (KWAD ran gul) - a four-sided enclosure surrounded by buildings

restored (re STORD) - renewed, returned to the original condition

secularize (SEHK u lar eyes) - to transfer from church to state control

INDEX

adobe bricks 7
Alamo, the 16, 18
Arizona 16, 28
Baja California 26
Bible 9
California
    11, 16, 20, 21, 22, 26, 28, 29
Caribbean Sea 11
Carmel, CA (mission at) 29
Christian natives 9, 21, 26
Christianity 5, 13, 26
churches 28
colonists 7, 13
Columbus, Christopher 5
crops 9
diseases 13, 22
England 7, 13, 14
English settlers 11, 13
European culture 21
festivals 28
Florida 11, 13, 14
forts 11, 20
France 7
Franciscan Monks, Order of 5
Georgia 11, 13
gold rush 22
heathens 9
La Purisima (Mission) 29
Lasuen, Father Fermin 20
Mexico 11, 16, 20, 21
Mission of Nuestra Senora 28
Mission of San Juan Capistrano 28, 29
mission natives 8, 26
Native Americans (natives) 5, 7, 8,
    9, 11, 13, 21, 22, 24, 26
New Mexico 16, 28
New Spain (see Mexico)
New World 5, 8, 9, 16

North America 5, 7, 8
padres (see priests)
Pecos, NM 28
plaza 7
Popé 16
presidios (see forts)
priests 5, 9, 11, 16, 20
Pueblo Revolt 16, 28
pueblos (see villages)
quadrangle 7
religion (religious beliefs) 8, 11
Roman Catholic Church 5, 8
Russia 20
St. Augustine, FL 13
St. Joseph's Day 28
Salinas Pueblo Missions National
    Monument 28
San Antonio de Valero (see Alamo)
San Antonio Missions National
    Historic Park 28
San Esteban (Mission) 28
San Xavier del Bac Mission 28
Santa Anna, General 16
secularization 16
Serra, Father Junipero 20, 26, 29
soldiers 11, 20, 26
Southeast 13, 14
Southwest 11, 16
Spain 5, 7, 8, 9, 11, 13, 14, 16, 20
Spanish culture 8
Spanish customs 5, 8, 24
Spanish settlers 16, 20
stone 7
Texas 16, 18, 28
Tumacacori National Historic Park 28
United States 7, 11, 21
villages 9